J
BIO
Deere

Hall, Margaret,
1947–
John Deere

SEP 27 2005		
MAR 03 2007		
OCT 11 2007		
NOV 25 2007		

Lives and Times

John Deere

M. C. Hall

Heinemann Library
Chicago, Illinois

Page layout by Cherylyn Bredemann
Map by John Fleck
Photo research by Julie Laffin

Printed and bound in Hong Kong and China by South China Printing Co Ltd

08 07 06 05 04
10 9 8 7 6 5 4 3 2 1

**Library of Congress
Cataloging-in-Publication Data**
John Deere / M. C. Hall.
ISBN 1-4034-5327-6 (HC), 1-4034-5335-7 (Pbk.)
The Cataloging-in-Publication Data for this title is on file with the Library of Congress.

Acknowledgments
The author and publishers are grateful to the following for permission to reproduce copyright material:
Title page, icon (tracker), pp. 4, 5, 10, 11, 12, 15, 16, 17, 18, 19, 20, 21, 22, 23, 24, 25, 26, 27, 28 Deere and Company Archives; icon (hay), p. 6 Corbis; p. 7 Hulton-Deutsch Collection/Corbis; p. 8 Culver Pictures, Inc.; p. 9 Gianni Dagli Orti/Corbis; p. 13 Bettmann/Corbis; p. 29 Rick Trahan/John Deere Historic Site Blacksmith

Cover photographs by Deere and Company Archives

The publisher would like to thank Charly Rimsa for her comments in the preparation of this book.

Every effort has been made to contact copyright holders of any material reproduced in this book. Any omissions will be rectified in subsequent printings if notice is given to the publisher.

Some words are shown in bold, **like this.** You can find out what they mean by looking in the glossary.

Contents

Farming for Food

For thousands of years, farmers have used tools to help them grow food. One of the first farm tools was the **iron** plow. It cut through the soil so seeds could be planted.

Farmers used horses or other animals to pull their plows.

John started a company that still makes farm tools today.

John Deere invented a plow that changed farming forever. His plow was made of **steel** instead of iron. It worked well in sticky, thick dirt.

The Early Years

John Deere was born on February 7, 1804, in Rutland, Vermont. John's father was a **tailor.** His mother was a **seamstress.** In 1805 the family moved to Middlebury, Vermont.

Vermont has thick forests and rolling hills.

These tanners are scraping animal skins to make leather.

When John was four years old, his father died. John's mother worked hard to support the family. John wanted to help out. He took a job helping a **tanner** after school.

Working and Learning

When he was seventeen years old, John became an **apprentice** to learn how to be a blacksmith. Blacksmiths made and fixed metal tools and small machines.

Blacksmiths made and fixed tools like these.

In return for his work, John had a bed, food, clothing, and a small **salary.** He was an apprentice for four years. Then, he worked as a blacksmith's helper.

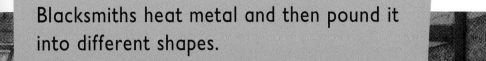

Blacksmiths heat metal and then pound it into different shapes.

A Blacksmith Shop

For several years John worked for other **blacksmiths.** Then, he bought land and built his own shop. In 1827 John married Demarius Lamb. He had met her while he was an **apprentice.**

This blacksmith is using a hammer to shape hot **steel.**

Flames from a blacksmith's fire could burn down a wooden building.

John's shop burned down twice in just a short period of time. It cost money to rebuild each time. He could not afford to keep rebuilding his shop. He had to find a new job.

Moving On

John took a job fixing **stagecoaches** and wagons. In 1833 he moved with his family to Hancock, Vermont. John built another **blacksmith** shop where he made tools, such as shovels and rakes.

This photograph shows John's shop in around 1927.

It was easier to raise sheep in Vermont than farm there.

Vermont's rocky soil made farming hard. Many farmers gave up farming. That meant there was less work for blacksmiths. In 1836 John moved west where there were many farmers who needed tools.

Settling in the West

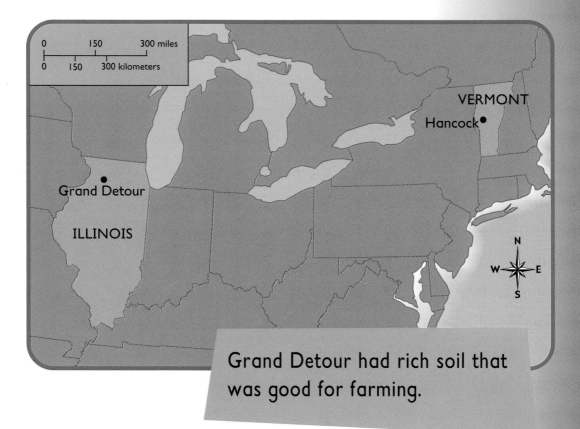

Grand Detour had rich soil that was good for farming.

John sold his **blacksmith** business in Vermont. Demarius could not travel because she was going to have a baby. So John went alone to Grand Detour, Illinois.

In Grand Detour, John built a blacksmith's shop. One of his first jobs was fixing a broken saw blade for a man named Leonard Andrus. John did such good work that other people hired him.

This was John's blacksmith shop in Grand Detour.

Plow Problems

Grand Detour was in the middle of the **prairie.** The soil was good, but it was hard to cut through the thick roots of the grass. The soil also stuck to **iron** plow blades.

Farmers had to stop often to clean off the plow blade.

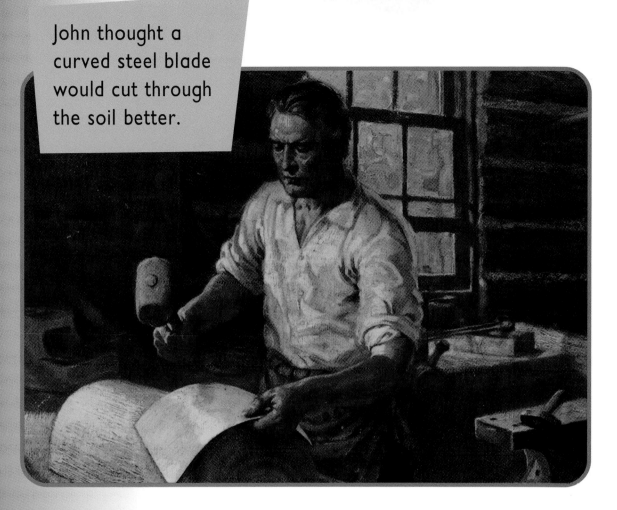

John thought a curved steel blade would cut through the soil better.

Some of John's **customers** told him about their problem. They said they needed a plow blade that would cut through the thick soil. John had an idea to make a plow with a **steel** blade.

A New Kind of Plow

The first plow John made is at the Smithsonian Museum in Washington, D.C.

John cut the teeth off a broken **steel** saw blade. Then, he heated the steel and bent it to make a curved blade. He put the blade on a wooden frame and added handles.

When John tried his new plow, it cut through the grass and dirt easily. The thick dirt slid off the curved steel blade. John started making and selling steel plows.

John tested his new plow in a friend's field.

The Company Grows

John's wife and children stayed in Vermont until after baby Charles was born. In 1838 Demarius and the five children came to Grand Detour. They moved into a house John had built for them.

This is the house where John and his family lived.

John and Leonard's company was called the L. Andrus Plough Manufactory. "Plough" is another way to spell plow.

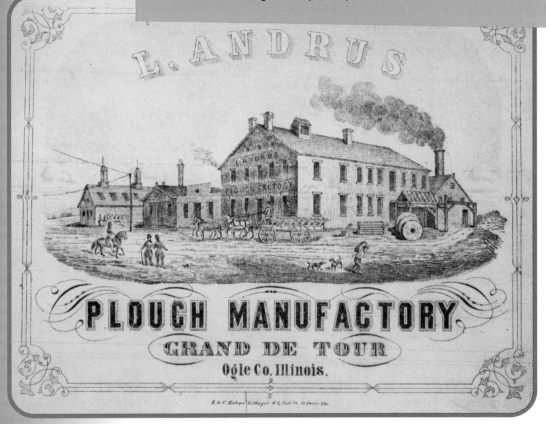

L. ANDRUS

PLOUGH MANUFACTORY

GRAND DE TOUR

Ogle Co. Illinois.

In 1842 John started a company to make steel plows. His company sold 100 plows that year. In 1843 John and Leonard Andrus became **business partners.**

A New Factory

In 1848 Leonard left to start his own company. John decided to move to Moline, Illinois, on the Mississippi River. There he found two new **business partners.** Their company built a new **factory.**

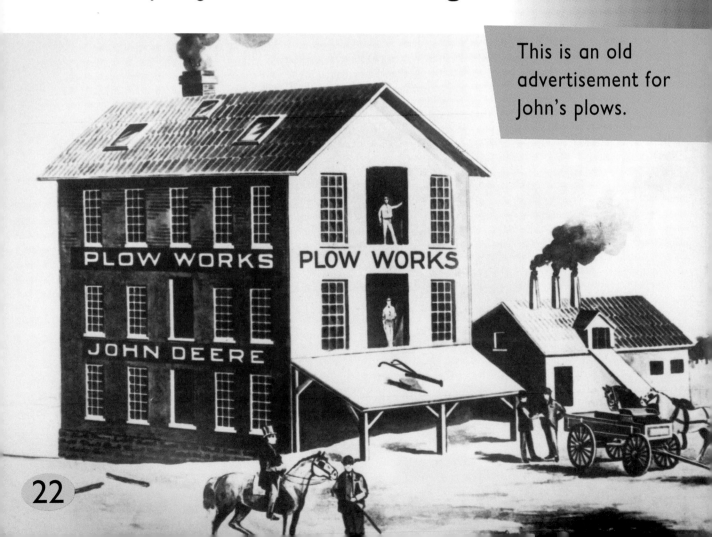

This is an old advertisement for John's plows.

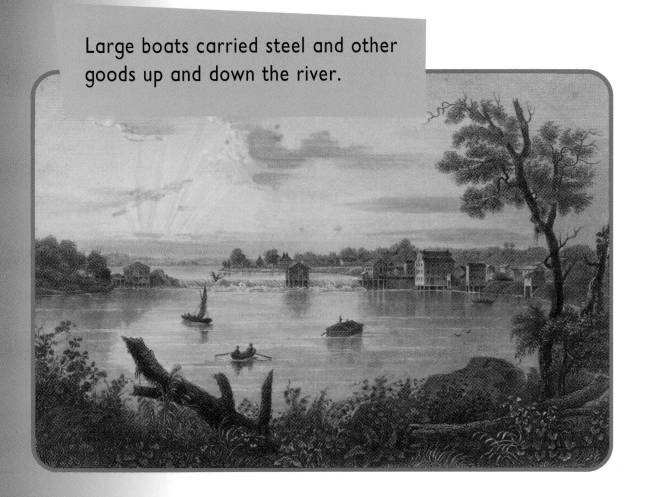

Large boats carried steel and other goods up and down the river.

Moline was a good place for a factory. The railroad ran through the city. Boats stopped there, too. That made it easier to get **steel** and to send finished plows to **customers** in other places.

Father and Son

The company was soon selling hundreds of plows every year. By 1852 John did not need **business partners.** He had enough money to run the company on his own. In 1853 his son Charles joined the company.

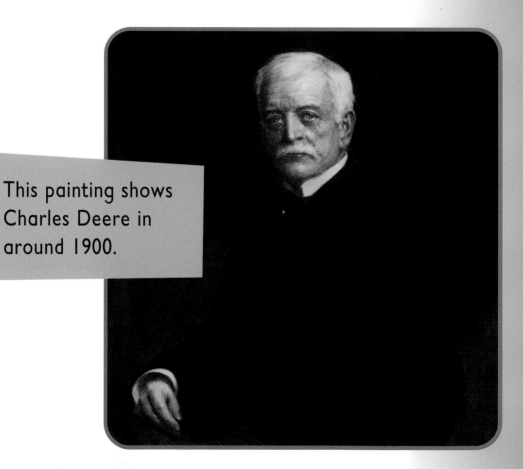

This painting shows Charles Deere in around 1900.

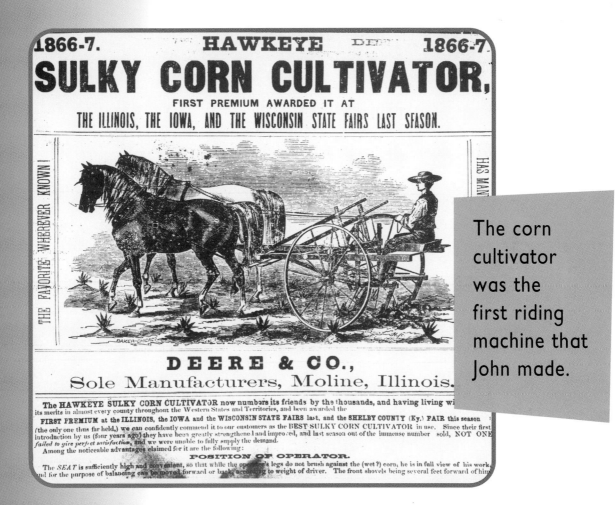

The corn cultivator was the first riding machine that John made.

Charles was a good salesperson. In 1858 John put him in charge of the **factory.** That gave John time to think of ideas for new machines. He also became a farmer and raised cows and pigs.

The Later Years

In 1865 Demarius died. John was lonely. He went back to Vermont to visit family. While he was there, he spent time with Demarius's sister, Lucenia. They were married in 1866.

Lucenia moved to Moline after she and John were married.

This photograph shows many workers at John's factory.

In 1873 John became the mayor of Moline.
He helped the town in other ways, too.
He gave money to schools and churches.
He helped new businesses get started.
In 1886 John died at the age of 82.

Learning More About John Deere

Today, there are John Deere **factories** in many different countries. The company makes and sells farm machines and lawn equipment around the world. John Deere machines are known for their quality.

This John Deere machine harvests grain.

The first plow John made is on display at the Smithsonian Museum in Washington, D.C. People can visit Grand Detour to see the house and shop where John once lived and worked.

This statue of John is at the John Deere Historic Site in Grand Detour.

Fact File

- John Deere & Company is one of the oldest manufacturing companies in the United States.

- John Deere always wanted to produce quality machines. He once said, "I will never put my name on a product that does not have in it the best that is in me."

- The farmer who owned the field where John tested his plow liked the machine so much that he bought one.

- John Deere machines are often green. People even call the green color the company uses "John Deere green."

Timeline

1804	John Deere is born.
1821	John begins work as an **apprentice blacksmith.**
1827	John marries Demarius Lamb.
1828	John and Demarius have a son, Francis. He is the first of nine children.
1829	John builds his first blacksmith shop in Leicester, Vermont.
1833	John builds another blacksmith shop in Hancock, Vermont.
1836	John leaves Vermont to settle in Grand Detour, Illinois.
1837	John makes a plow with a **steel** blade.
1848	John moves his family and business to Moline, Illinois.
1853	Charles, John's oldest living son, joins the business.
1858	John puts Charles in charge of the company.
1865	Demarius Deere dies.
1866	John marries Lucenia Lamb, Demarius's sister.
1886	John Deere dies.

Glossary

apprentice   person who learns a job by working with someone who is an expert

blacksmith   person who makes and fixes things with iron

business partner   person who works with someone else to run a business

customer   person who buys a product

factory   place where a product is made

iron   rough metal found in the soil

prairie   flat, grassy land with good soil

salary   pay for doing a job

seamstress   woman who earns money by sewing for other people

stagecoach   carriage drawn by horses that carried people and mail

steel   shiny metal made from iron that is heated until it melts

tailor   person who earns money by making clothing

tanner   person who turns animal skins into leather

More Books to Read

An older reader can help you with these books:

Collins, David R. *Pioneer Plowmaker: A Story About John Deere.* Minneapolis, Minn.: Carolrhoda, 2003.

Harrington, Roy. *Grandpa's John Deere Tractors.* Saint Joseph, Mich.: American Society of Agricultural Engineers, 1996.

Marsh, Carole. *John Deere.* Peachtree City, Ga.: Gallopode, 2002.